Intro to Polyrhythms
Contracting and Expanding Time Within Form

by Ari Hoenig & Johannes Weidenmueller

Vol. 1

Video
dv.melbay.com/21108

You Tube
www.melbay.com/21108V

2 3 4 5 6 7 8 9 0

© 2009 BY MEL BAY PUBLICATIONS, INC., PACIFIC, MO 63069.
ALL RIGHTS RESERVED. INTERNATIONAL COPYRIGHT SECURED. B.M.I. MADE AND PRINTED IN U.S.A.
No part of this publication may be reproduced in whole or in part, stored in a retrieval system, or transmitted in any form
or by any means, electronic, mechanical, photocopy, recording, or otherwise, without written permission of the publisher.

Visit us on the Web at www.melbay.com — E-mail us at email@melbay.com

contents

Introduction 3

Explanation of Terms 4

Practice Tips 5

Eighth-Note Triplets 8

Eighth Notes 10

Quarter-Note Triplets in 4/4 14

Dotted Quarter Notes in 3/4 19

Dotted Quarter Notes in 4/4 23

Core Grooves 25

Displacing the Harmonic Rhythm 27

Chord Progressions 32

Suggested Listening 35

About the Authors 36

introduction

Welcome to Volume I of our **Intro to Polyrhythms: Contracting and Expanding Time within Form**

So you are curious about polyrhythms, about the language and vocabulary of metric modulation and superimposition? Maybe you only have a vague idea what these concepts mean and would like to know more. Or you've always wanted to incorporate more rhythmic freedom into your playing but are not quite sure how to develop this skill. Maybe you recently found yourself in a musical situation in which you felt rhythmically unprepared. Whatever your reasons are, you've come to the right place. We will attempt to demystify the subject and present you with a codified approach to learning the vocabulary and language of metric modulation and superimposition.

This language is nothing new. Polyrhythms such as three against two and four against three have been part of the African music tradition for many centuries, and polyrhythms have always been an integral part of the jazz tradition.

The Miles Davis Quintet of the 1960's was one of the first jazz ensembles to explore and develop a language based on this vocabulary. The result was an amazing freedom within form. In the last decade or two, the use of metric modulation in jazz has increased exponentially: Polyrhythmic vocabulary has become very sophisticated, and it is rare to hear a jazz ensemble perform original music that does not employ it in one way or another. It has become so common that the ability to understand and apply time shifts and modulations has in fact become a fundamental skill, a skill that in our opinion every serious jazz musician should acquire to some degree.

We have found that there are very few educational materials available that address the subject as a whole, and those who do are almost exclusively geared towards drummers.

The material on this video addresses all instrumentalists and presents a comprehensive approach to understanding and applying the language of polyrhythms, metric modulation and superimposition within a jazz context.

The text and notational examples should be referred to if necessary only after listening to and trying to absorb the musical examples by ear. The idea is that these musical examples should be learned primarily aurally, in an organic way. This process will aid you in making musical decisions that are dictated by emotion and not by mathematics.

Ari and Johannes

terms

Here is a quick explanation of some of the terms we are using:

Metric Modulation

In technical terms, metric modulation signifies changing the tempo of a piece so that the new tempo has some kind of mathematical relation to the original tempo. This is achieved by making a note value from the first tempo equivalent to a note value in the second. For example if you take a half note in your original tempo and make that half note equal to the quarter note in the new tempo you end up with a modulation to halftime.

Superimposed Metric Modulation

On this video we are applying all the modulations over a form, in which the original harmonic structure and time feel stay intact. Therefore we are actually superimposing one time feel or pulse over another. **Polyrhythms** are a good example of this. The superimposed or layered pulse or what we call **core rhythm** and **core groove** create the illusion of the tempo momentarily shifting when in fact it is not. So, technically speaking, most of the examples on this video are superimposed metric modulations, but for the sake of simplicity we will stick with the term "metric modulation".

Core Rhythms

Subdivisions such as eighth notes, triplets and sixteenth notes can be grouped to form what we call a **core rhythm**. For instance, a dotted quarter note is a **core rhythm**; it is based on the subdivision of eighth notes in groupings of three. There are three basic **core rhythms** that we explore in Volume I: dotted quarter-notes, eighth-note triplets and quarter-note triplets. **Core rhythms** are the basic building blocks for what we call **core grooves.**

Core Grooves

Core grooves are a more musical application of **core rhythms**. To create a core groove, first we take a **core rhythm** and play it in groupings of two, three, four or five etc... Examples of **core grooves** include a basic swing, samba or bossa that is superimposed over a different time feel.

Forms

There are a few reasons why we think it is more beneficial to apply these exercises over a form rather than just over a particular pulse. First of all, one of the purposes of superimposing one groove or time feel over another is to create tension. Rhythmic superimposition creates two sets of pulses competing for your attention and therefore two sets of competing musical expectations. A form - any cyclical set of bars, with or without harmonic movement - provides an opportunity to raise the intensity of your expectations for resolution. Without a form over which to apply the new groove, you won't achieve the same amount of tension nor the effect of any subsequent release. Second of all, in order for musicians to communicate with one another, we must have some kind of a framework or road map as a basis of communication. A form can be that framework. The ultimate purpose of the exercises in this book is to help you navigate chord progressions and form in a musical way. The forms that we are playing over are a twelve-bar blues in 4/4, a twelve-bar blues in 3/4, rhythm changes, and a 32-bar AABA form.

Rhythmic Displacements

A rhythmic displacement is any rhythm or musical phrase that begins on a different part of the beat than its original starting point. This video covers rhythmic displacement extensively as well as polyrhythms and metric modulation.

practice tips

General Practice Tips

Before you start playing any of these exercises on your instrument you should be able to clap, speak or sing them first. This helps you isolate the exercises and eliminates factors that could interfere, such as note choices or other technical aspects of your instrument etc.

There are many different ways to practice these exercises. Keep in mind that no matter what core rhythm or groove you are displacing or superimposing, the original time (eighth note, quarter note or half note) has to stay your reference point.

At the begining you might find it necessary to maintain an external reference point for the original time such as a metronome, a recording that you play along with or a fellow musician who is willing to keep time for you. As you get more comfortable, your dependance on an external time keeper will diminish and you will be able to rely more and more on your internal metronome.

Here are some suggestions for practicing the exercises away from your instrument:

1. Clap the core rhythm while keeping the metronome on all four beats of every bar.

2. Clap the core rhythm while keeping the metronome on beats two and four of every bar.

3. Clap the core rhythm while keeping the metronome on beat one of every bar.

4. Replace the metronome with tapping your foot and repeat the above exercises.

5. Sing or speak the core rhythm while clapping all four beats of every bar.

6. Sing or speak the core rhythm while clapping on beats two and four of every bar.

7. Sing or speak the core rhythm while clapping on beat one of every bar.

8. When you're walking, think of your steps as half notes or quarter notes. While doing this, clap your hands or sing the core rhythm.

For 3/4 time adjust the above exercises accordingly.

practice tips for drummers

While learning the examples in this book, it is helpful to keep the quarter-note pulse with either the hi-hat or bass drum. This is good for coordination as well as rhythmic understanding.

Be creative. Improvise within the core rhythm. Try playing the quarter-note pulse with two limbs while playing the core rhythm with the other two limbs. Try alternating these patterns between each pair of limbs. Then try playing the quarter note with one limb while the other three limbs play the core rhythm.

Drum Key

cymbal   hi-hat   hi-hat with foot   bass drum   snare

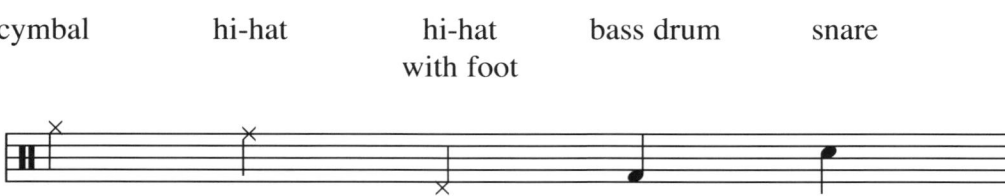

practice tips for bass players

We found that there is a tendency to play shorter notes when they are anticipated or delayed, particularly when it comes to the core rhythm of walking bass. In order to create the illusion of the time shifting temporarily, it is important that you play the full note values.

As a bass player, you must not only superimpose a core rhythm over a form - which is challenging enough - but at the same time you must displace the harmonic rhythm. Expressing the harmonic structure of a piece when the bass notes don't fall on beats one or three is not easy. If you find that you are having trouble with this see if the following suggestions help:

First, play the core rhythm or groove against a metronomic pulse making sure that you are completely secure with that. Then add the form but stay on one pitch and don't worry about expressing the harmony yet. Check to make sure you are hearing the form in your head. Finally add the harmonies. If you are unsure about where the chords fall in the new harmonic rhythm, write out a few choruses and consult the examples later in the book.

practice tips for pianists

All of the exercises and ideas presented in this book can be applied to comping as well as to soloing. Many pianists have limited independence of the right and left hand, and it is not uncommon that the left hand will follow the right hand or vice versa. Here are some suggestions on how to develop more independence while working with the core rhythms in this book.

Preliminary exercises

Pick a chord and voicing that are you are comfortable with (either left hand or two-handed voicing) and stick with it.

1. Play the core rhythm while keeping the metronome on all four beats of every bar.

2. Play the core rhythm while keeping the metronome on beats two and four of every bar.

3. Play the core rhythm while keeping the metronome on beat one of every bar.

4. Replace the metronome by tapping your foot and repeat the above exercises.

If you are comfortable with this, repeat the exercises while playing them over a form. Adding the element of form can get pretty challenging, particularly if the core rhythm goes over the bar-line and therefore changes the harmonic rhythm. Choose a chord progression that you are really comfortable and familiar with. The less you have to worry about finding the right notes or chords the better. You can find some suggestions on how to approach the subject in the chapter about harmonic rhythm.

Left and right-hand independence using the core rhythms.

Pick a chord and a left-hand voicing that you are comfortable with, and a scale in the right hand that fits with that chord.

1. With your left hand, comp on all four beats of the bar and play the core rhythm with your right hand using notes of the scale.

2. With your left hand, comp on beats two and four of the bar and play the core rhythm with your right hand using notes of the scale.

3. With your left hand, comp on beats one and three of the bar and play the core rhythm with your right hand using notes of the scale.

4. With your left hand, pick a standard comping rhythm and play the core rhythm with your right hand.

Reverse the exercises.

1. With your left hand, comp using the core rhythm and with your right hand play half notes using notes of the scale.

2. With your left hand, comp using the core rhythm and with your right hand play quarter notes using notes of the scale.

3. With your left hand, comp using the core rhythm and with your right hand play eighth notes using notes of the scale.

Next repeat the exercises but play them over a form. Again, choose something that you are really comfortable and familiar with. The more advanced you get the more you can experiment with making up your own exercises. Try to play the melody of a tune in your right hand while comping core rhythms in your left. You could combine two core rhythms, for example: solo using the core rhythm of quarter-note triplets in your right hand, and comp on every second triplet in your left. The possibilities are endless.

eighth-note triplets

This chapter deals with the core rhythm of eighth-note triplets. It is essential in all triplet-based music, such as swing, that you are able to feel equally comfortable on all three parts of the triplet. If you don't have this foundation set, all subsequent metric modulations based on triplets are going to be shaky and insecure, so make sure you really have these exercises down before you move on.

The form we are using for the exercises in this chapter is a 12–bar blues in the key of F.

Watch **Chapter 1** on the DVD to see how eighth-note triplet modulations can be applied in a musical way.

DVD Chapter 3: First note of the triplet

Core Rhythm

etc.

A quick note: the first note of the triplet is obviously the downbeat of every quarter-note, and while this might seem deceptively simple, it is not. Just playing quarter notes while keeping good time and swinging hard is more difficult then you think, and should be the foundation for any more complicated and advanced patterns.

Core Groove A: 4/4 Swing

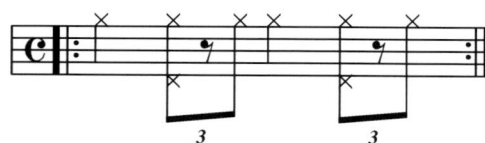

Basic Walking Core Groove

etc.

DVD Chapter 4: Third note of the triplet

Core Rhythm

etc.

DVD Chapter 5: Starting on the third note of the triplet

Core Groove A: Swing

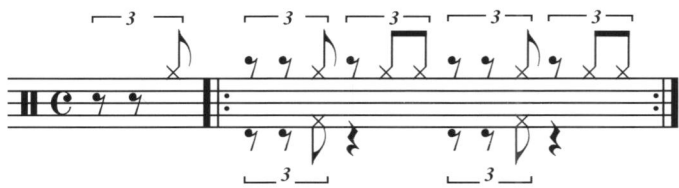

DVD Chapter 6: Second note of the triplet

Core Rhythm

DVD Chapter 7: Starting on the second note of the triplet

Core Groove A: Swing

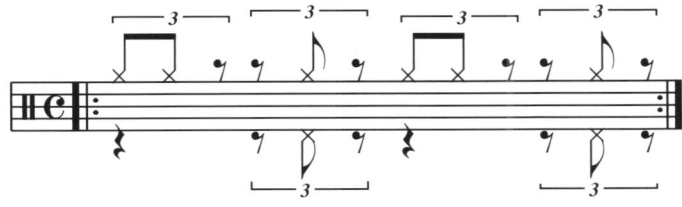

DVD Chapter 8: Aaron demonstrates on the piano how to solo using the second and third notes of the triplet.

eighth notes

This chapter deals with the core rhythm of an eighth note. Again, you want to feel equally comfortable on all eighth notes in a bar. This is the prerequisite to more complicated metric modulations. The form we are using in this chapter is rhythm changes in the key of B flat.

Watch **Chapter 9** on the DVD and see the trio apply the material in this chapter over "Rhythm Changes".

Core Rhythms

First eighth note on One and Three.

DVD Chapter 11: Second eighth note on the and of One and Three.

DVD Chapter 13: Third eighth note on Two and Four

DVD Chapter 15: Fourth eighth note on the and of Two and Four.

You can also think of these exercises as a grouping of four eighth notes that is being displaced by an eighth note.

Core Groove B: Half-Time Swing Feel

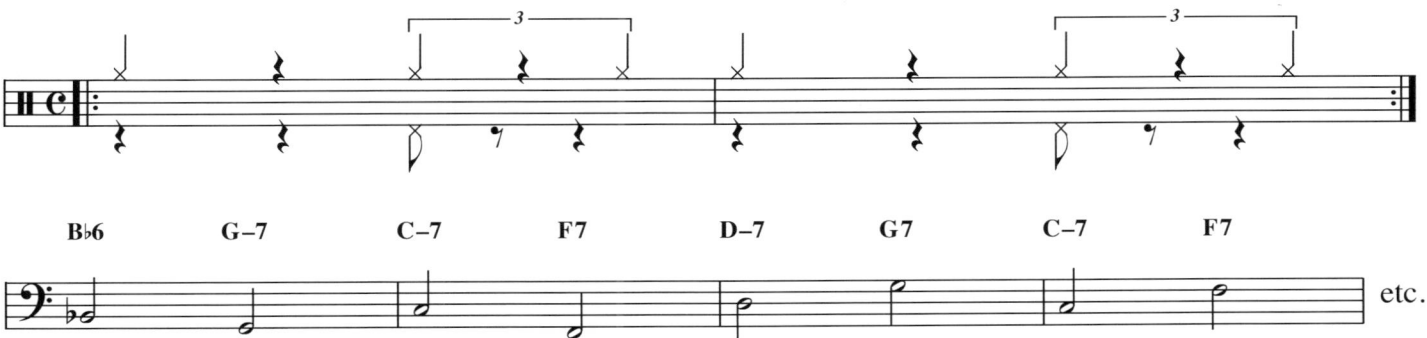

DVD Chapter 12: Core Groove B displaced by one eighth starting on the second eighth note. Eighth notes are swung.

DVD Chapter 14: Core Groove B displaced by a quarter note starting on the third eighth note.

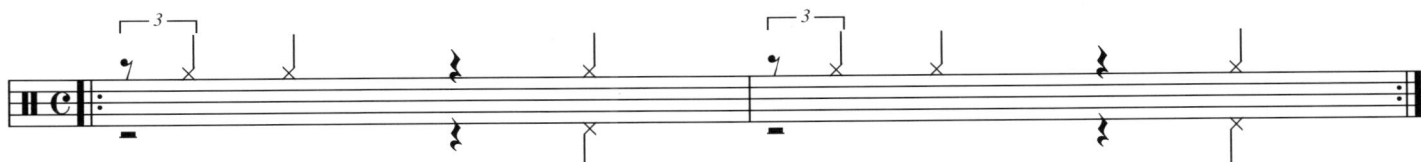

As a harmonic instrument you have the option of either anticipating or delaying the harmonic rhythm. Both work: just be aware that anticipating the harmonic rhythm will create a sense of forward motion.

For bass, delaying the harmonic rhythm looks like the following example:

Whereas anticipating looks like the following example:

DVD Chapter 16: Core Groove B displaced by three eighths starting on the fourth eighth note.

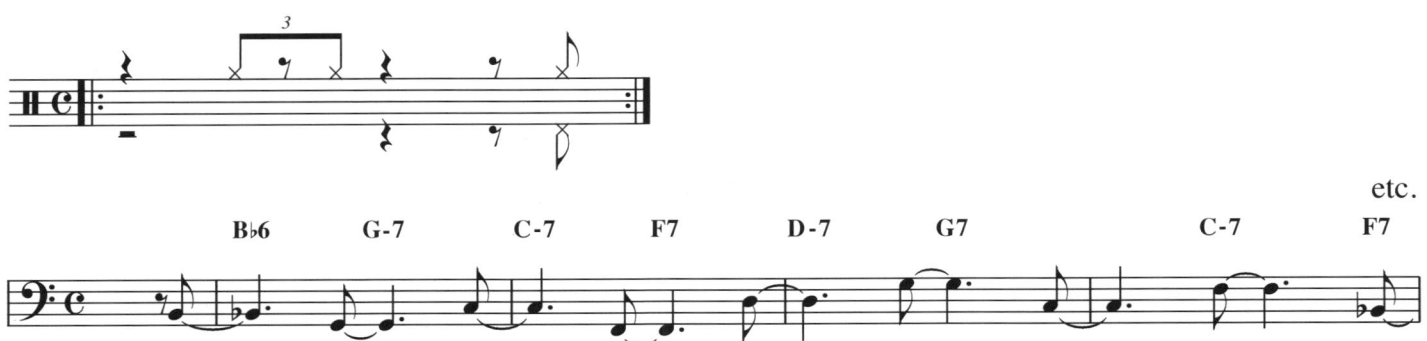

DVD Chapters 17, 18 and 19: Aaron demonstrates on the piano how to apply the second, third and fourth eighth note displacement while soloing over "Rhythm Changes".

DVD Chapters 20, 21 and 22: Here the trio demonstrates the musical application of the second, third and fourth eighth note displacement over "Rhythm Changes".

Below is an example of a simple funk groove displaced in the same manner.

Core Groove C: Funk

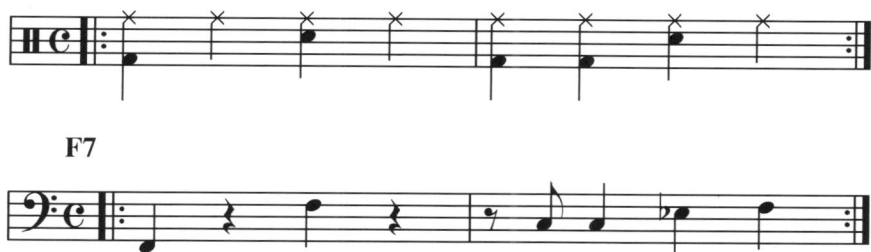

Displaced by one eighth note starting on the second eighth note.

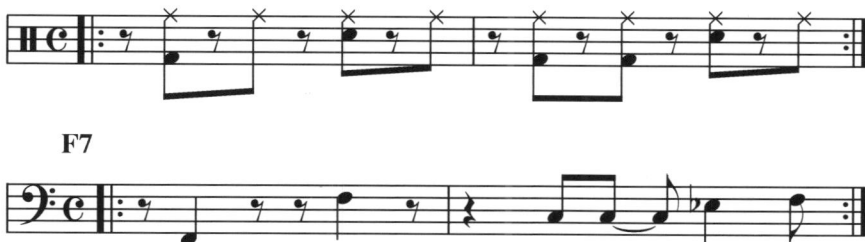

Displaced by a quarter note starting on the third eighth note.

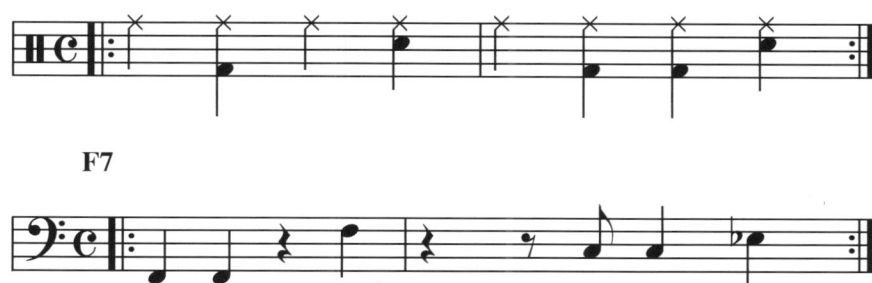

Displaced by three eighth notes starting on the fourth eighth note.

quarter-note triplets in 4/4

This chapter deals with the core rhythm of a quarter-note triplet.

If you are not completely comfortable with playing quarter-note triplets, go back to eighth-note triplets and make sure you are comfortable with those first. Eighth-note triplets are the building blocks for quarter-note triplets.

The form we are using for this chapter is a 4/4 blues in F.

Watch **Chapter 23** on the DVD and see the trio apply the material in this chapter over a blues.

Core Rhythm

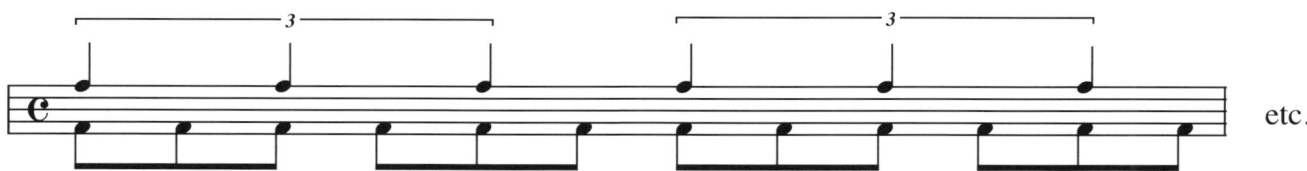

Take a basic eighth-note triplet pattern and accent every other note. The pattern repeats after six eighth-note triplets or two quarter notes.

DVD Chapter 25: Quarter-note triplet starting on beat One.

In 4/4 time, the pattern repeats after one bar.

Core Rhythm

DVD Chapter 26: Quarter-note triplet starting on the second eighth-note triplet (you can also think of it as starting on beat Two or beat Four).

Core Rhythm

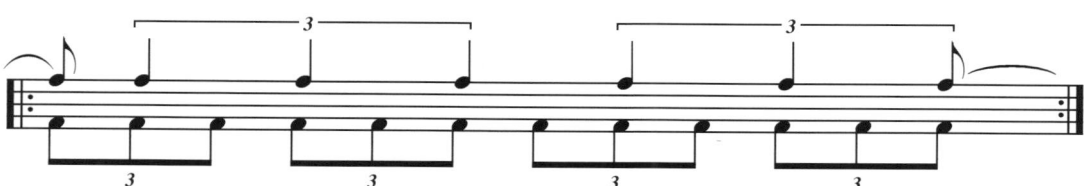

As a bass player you have the choice to either anticipate or delay the harmonic rhythm. Anticipating chords - in this case playing the chord change on the and of beat Four as opposed to on the second eighth-note triplet of beat One - gives the bass line a nice forward motion.

DVD Chapter 27: Quarter-note triplets grouped in twos.

Core Rhythm

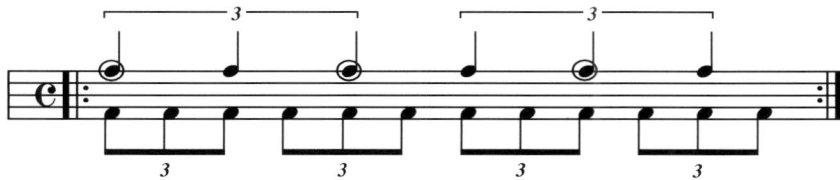

Core Groove A: Swing

DVD Chapter 28: Quarter-note triplets grouped in threes.

Core Rhythm

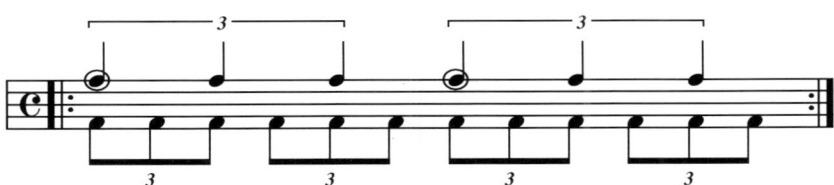

Core Groove D: 3/4 Swing

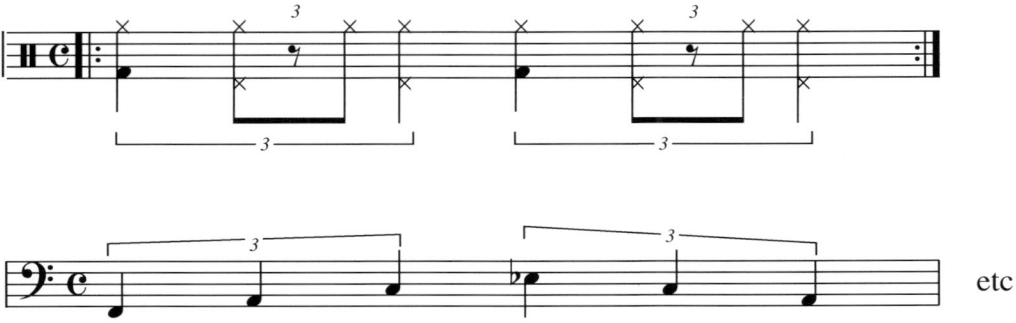

DVD Chapter 29: Quarter-note triplets grouped in fours.

Core Rhythm

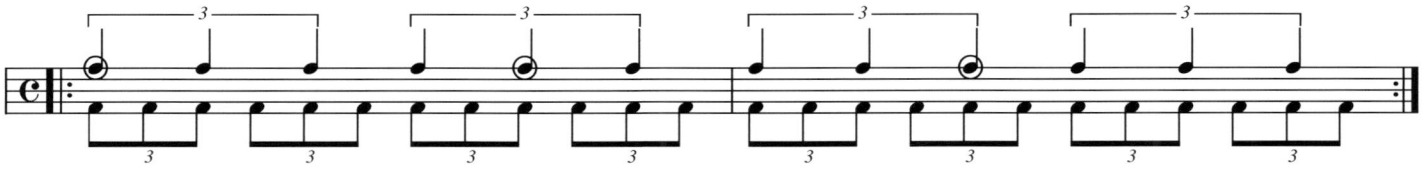

Core Groove F: Bossa

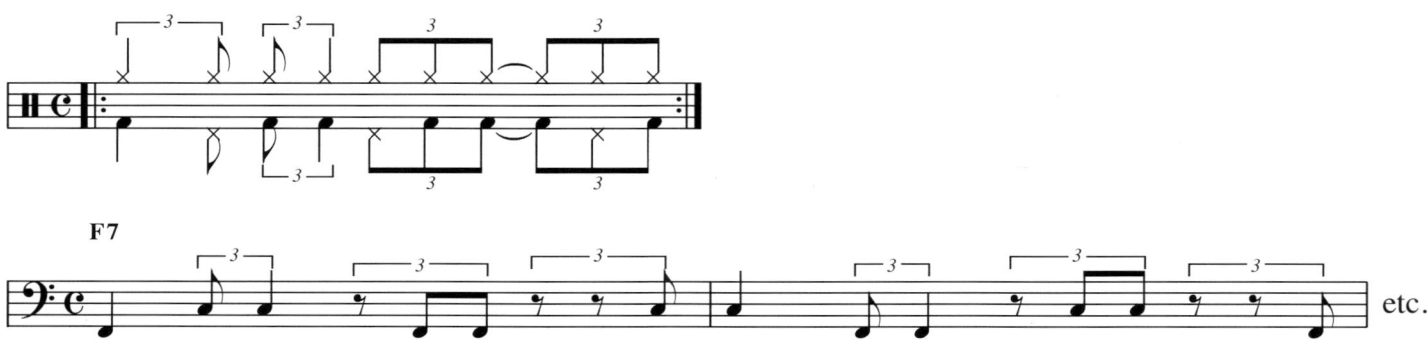

DVD Chapter 30: Here the trio demonstrates musical applications of quarter-note triplets over a blues.

DVD Chapter 31: Displaced quarter-note triplets in groupings of two.

Core Rhythm

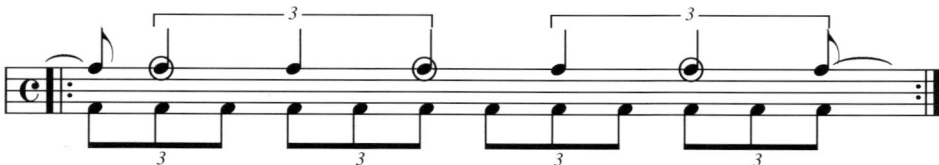

Core Groove C: Funk

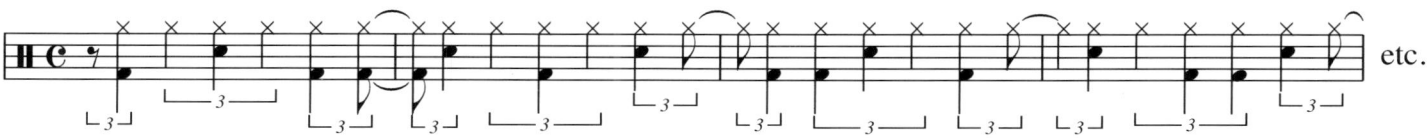

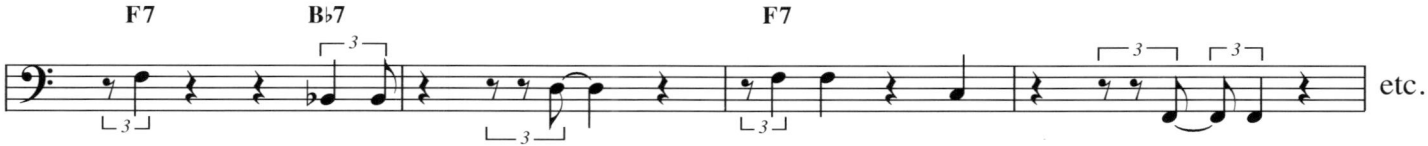

DVD Chapter 32: Displaced quarter-note triplets in groupings of three.

Core Rhythm

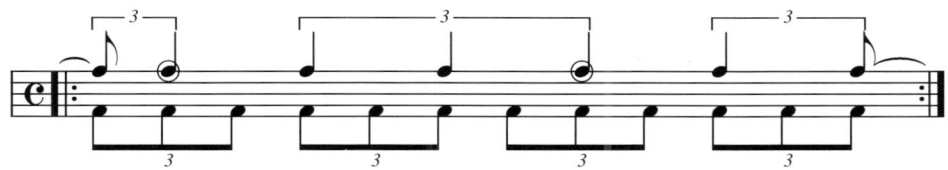

DVD Chapter 33: Displaced quarter-note triplets in groupings of three.

Core Groove D: 3/4 Swing

also: Displaced quarter-note triplets in groupings of three.

Core Groove E: Slow Blues in 3/4

etc.

DVD Chapter 34: Displaced quarter-note triplets in groupings of four.

Core Rhythm

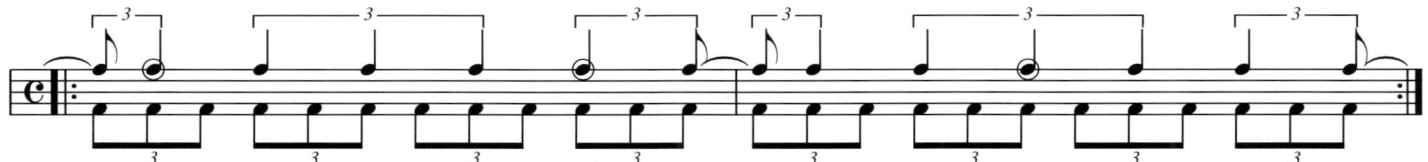

Core Groove A: Swing

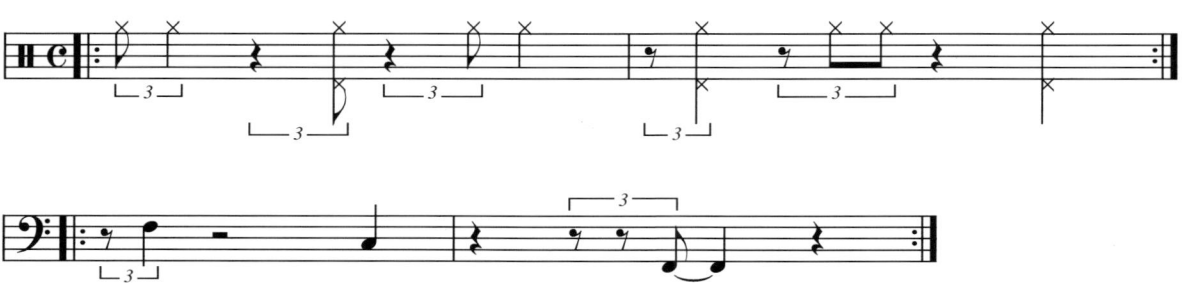

DVD Chapter 35: Here the trio demonstrates musical applications of displaced quarter-note triplets over a blues.

dotted quarter notes in 3/4

This chapter deals with the core rhythm of dotted quarter notes in 3/4.

Dotted quarter notes are eighth notes grouped in threes.

The form we are using for this chapter is a 24-bar C minor blues in 3/4.

Watch **Chapter 36** on the DVD and see the trio apply the material in this chapter over the tune "Pawprints".

DVD Chapter 38: Dotted quarter notes starting on beat One.

Core Rhythm

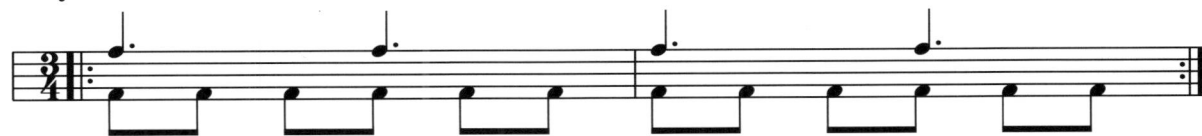

DVD Chapter 40: Dotted quarter notes starting on the 'and' of beat One.

Core Rhythm

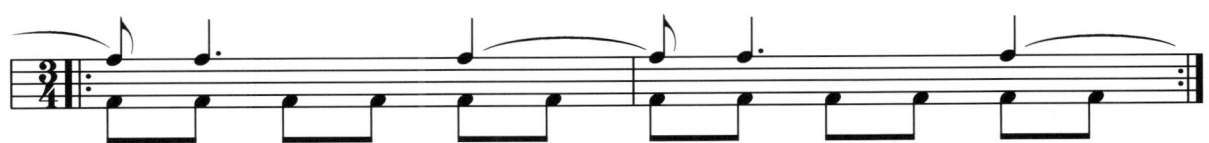

DVD Chapter 42: Dotted quarter notes starting on beat Two.

Core Rhythm

DVD Chapter 39: Dotted quarter notes grouped in twos.

Core Groove A: Swing

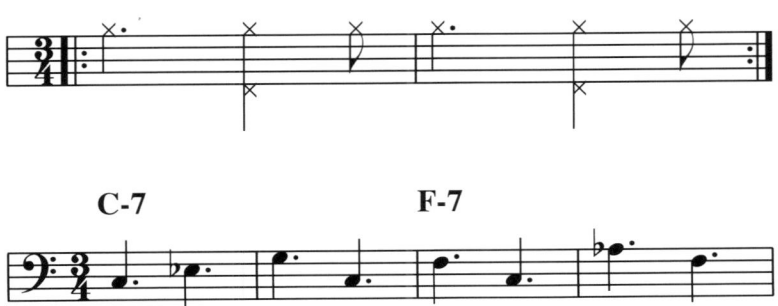

DVD Chapter 41: Dotted quarter notes grouped in twos starting on the 'and' of One.

Core Groove A: Swing

Note: The harmonic rhythm can either be delayed by an eighth note;

or can be anticipated by a quarter note.

DVD Chapter 43: Dotted quarter notes grouped in twos starting on beat Two.

Core Groove A: Swing

Again the harmonic rhythm can either be delayed by a quarter note

or it can be anticipated by and eighth note.

DVD Chapter 44: Dotted quarter notes grouped in threes.

Core Rhythm

Note: Accent every third dotted quarter note.

DVD Chapter 45: Dotted quarter notes grouped in threes.

Core Groove D: 3/4 Swing

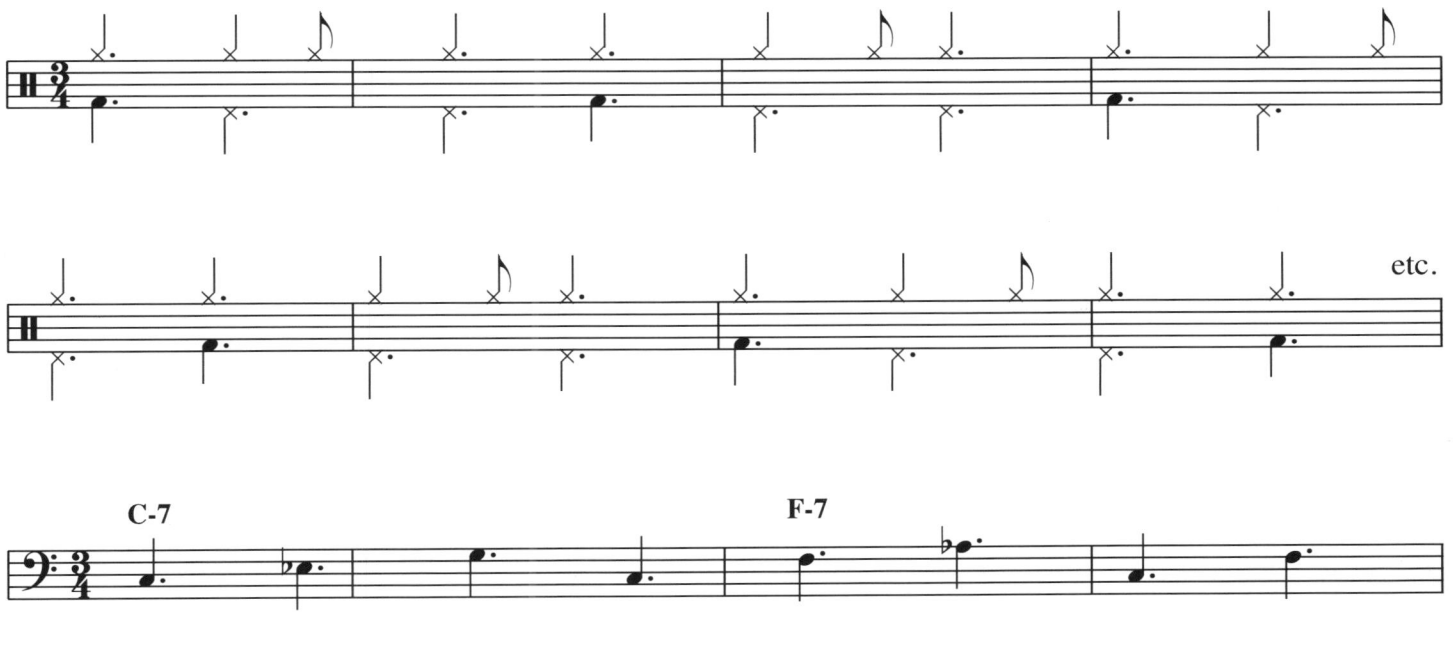

DVD Chapter 46: Dotted quarter notes grouped in threes starting on the 'and' of One.

Core Rhythm

DVD Chapter 47: Dotted quarter notes grouped in threes starting on the 'and' of One.

Core Groove D: 3/4 Swing

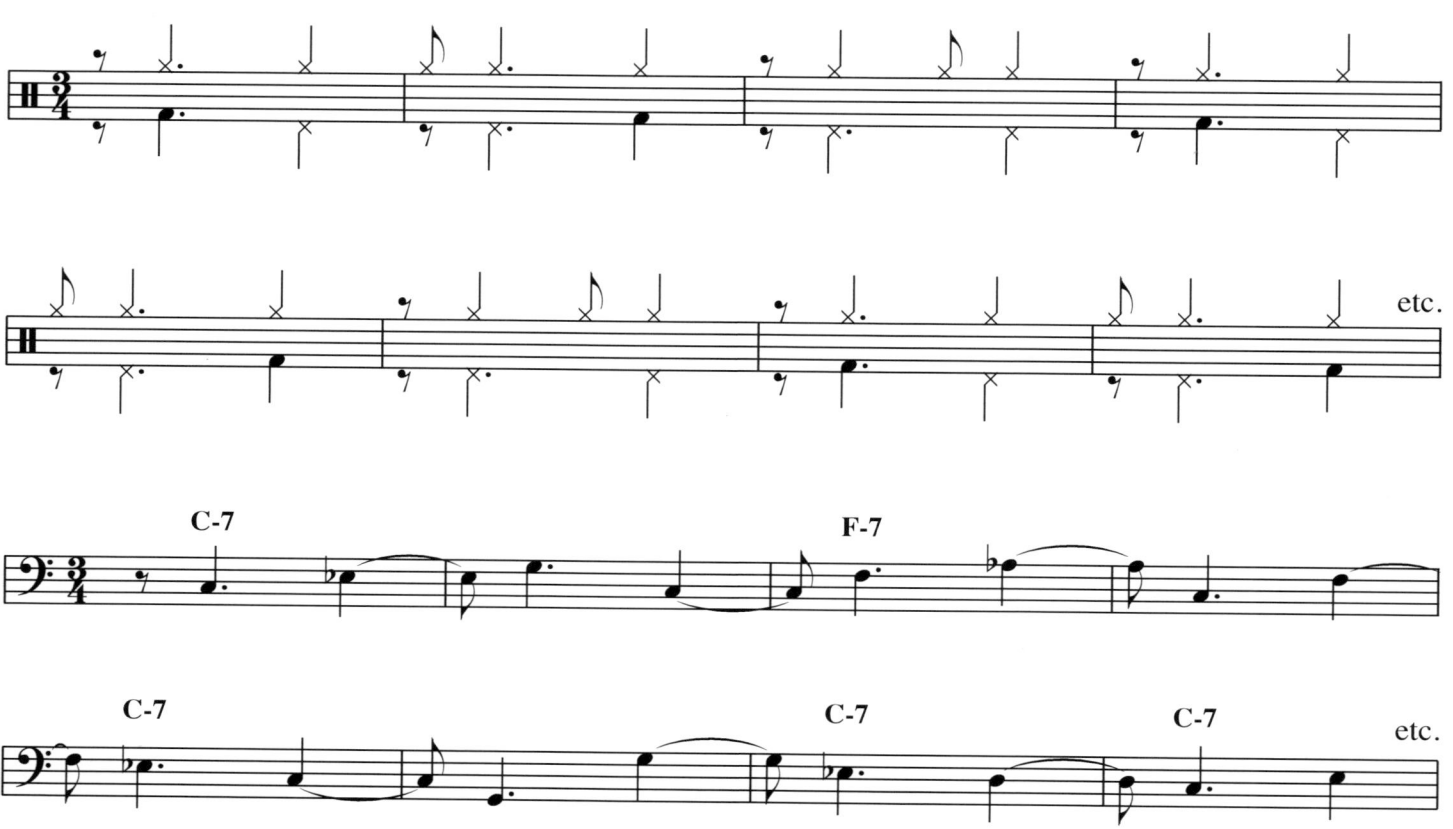

DVD Chapter 48: The trio demonstrates dotted quarters starting on One.

DVD Chapter 49: The trio demonstrates dotted quarters starting on the 'and' of One.

dotted quarter-notes in 4/4

This chapter deals with the core rhythm of dotted quarter notes in 4/4. There are two dotted quarter notes for every three quarter notes and in 4/4 the pattern repeats after three bars. The form we are using for this chapter is a typical 32 bar AABA form. Watch **Chapter 50** on the DVD and see the trio apply the material in this chapter over the tune "Take the G Train".

DVD Chapter 52: Dotted quarter notes in 4/4

Core Rhythm

DVD Chapter 53: Dotted quarter notes grouped in twos.

Core Groove A: Swing

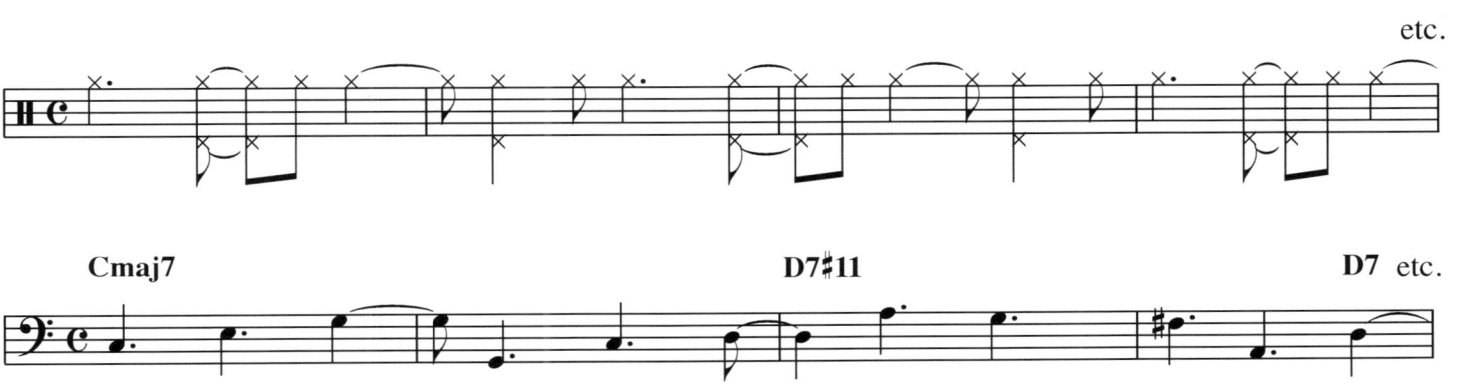

DVD Chapter 54: Dotted quarter notes grouped in threes.

Core Rhythm

Note: Accent every third dotted quarter-note. This rhythm repeats after nine bars.

DVD Chapter 55: Dotted quarter notes grouped in threes.

Core Groove D: Swing in 3/4

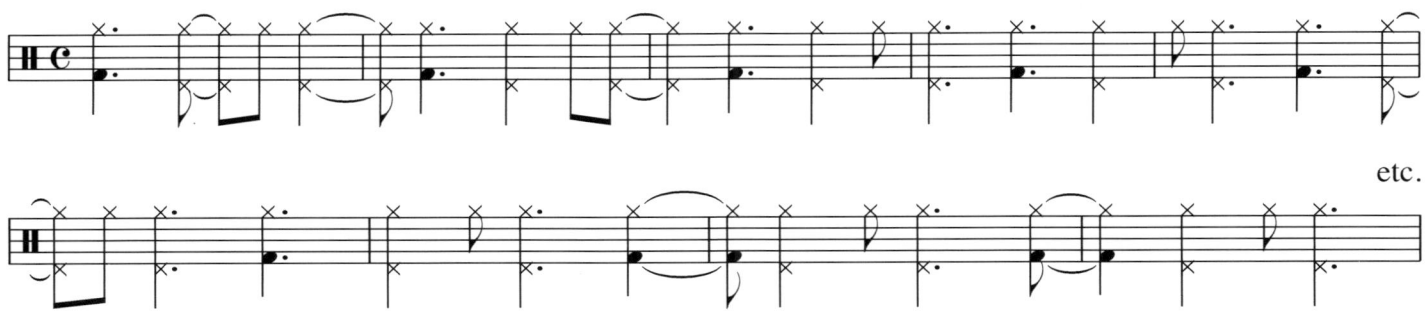

Note: Pattern repeats after 9 bars.

The following are some more examples of core grooves of dotted quarter notes grouped in fours.

Core Groove C: Funk

Dotted quarter notes grouped in fours starting on the 'and' of One.

DVD Chapter 56: Trio demonstrates dotted quarter notes in 4/4 time.

core grooves

Here is a listing of the core grooves we are using on the DVD

Core Groove A: 4/4 Swing

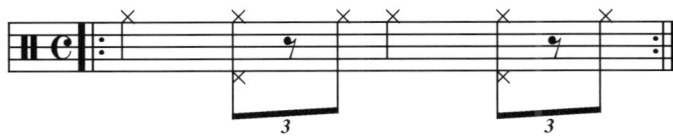

Core Groove B: Halftime Swing

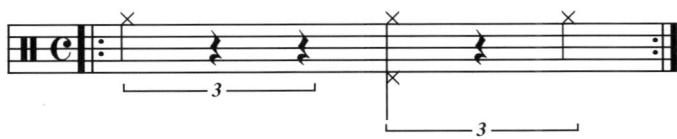

Core Groove C: 4/4 Funk

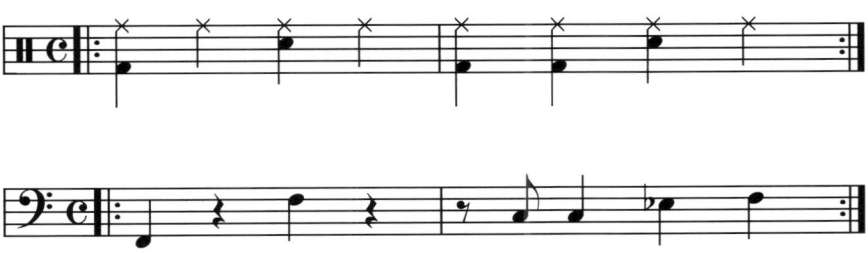

Core Groove D: 3/4 Swing

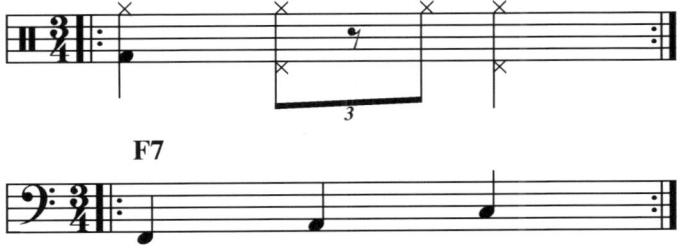

or

F7

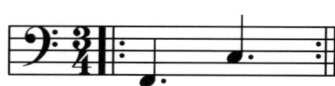

Core Groove E: 3/4 Slow Blues

F7

Core Groove F: Bossa

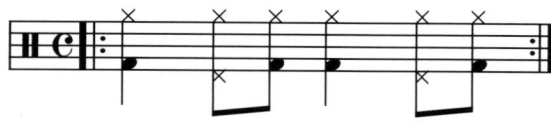

F7

displacing the harmonic rhythm

Some of the previous exercises involve displacing the harmonic rhythm. When you apply a core rhythm such as a dotted quarter note to a harmonic structure, the harmonic rhythm will be displaced and chords will no longer fall only on beat One or beats One and Three. Sometimes there will not be enough beats in the new time to express all the chords, and sometimes there will be too many beats and you will have to repeat chords. You have to try to fit the new rhythm over the existing harmonic structure/form and make it sound musical. Often times you are faced with having to either anticipate or delay the harmony; both work. Anticipating the harmony will give the tune a feeling of forward motion, whereas delaying it will give it a feeling of stretching the time.

Here is an example of a dotted quarter harmonic rhythm over an F blues in 4/4. The chord changes that do not fall on beat One or Three are anticipated.

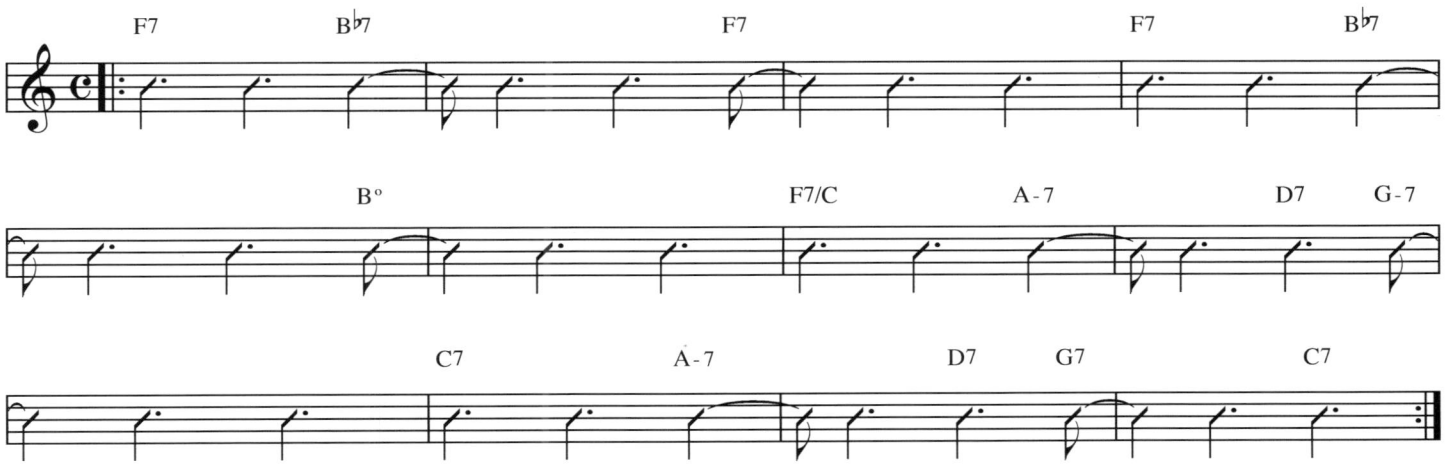

This is what a bass line for the above example could look like.

Here is another way of playing the harmonic rhythm. Some of the chords are now delayed.

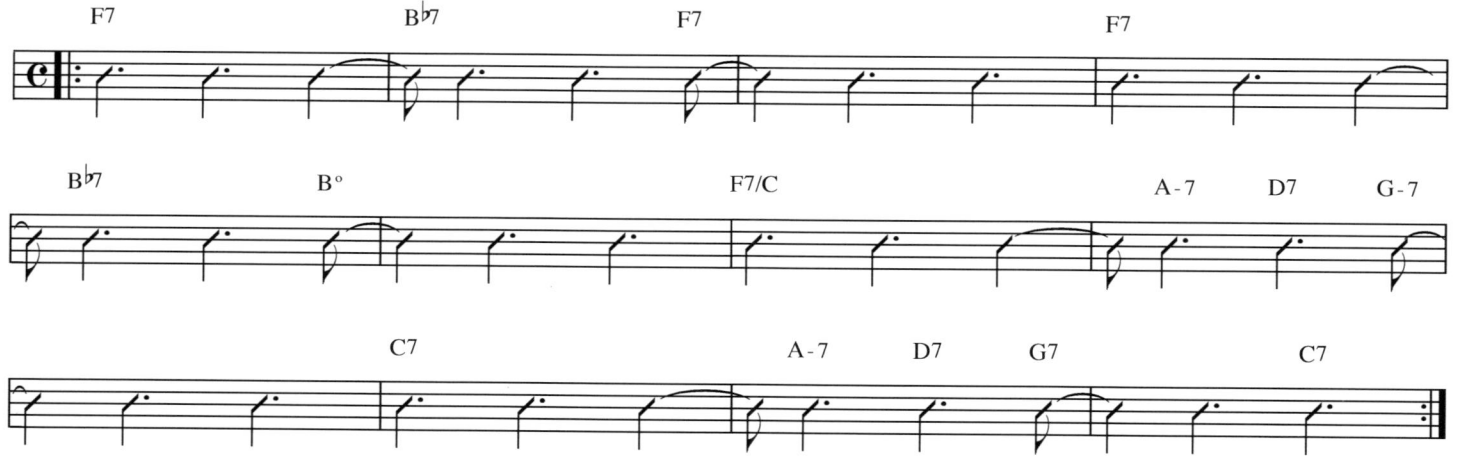

This is what a bass line could look like for the above example.

Notice that the basic rhythmic pattern repeats after three bars.

Here is a dotted quarter core rhythm over the chord changes to "Take the G Train", a typical 32 bar, AABA form.

Take the G Train

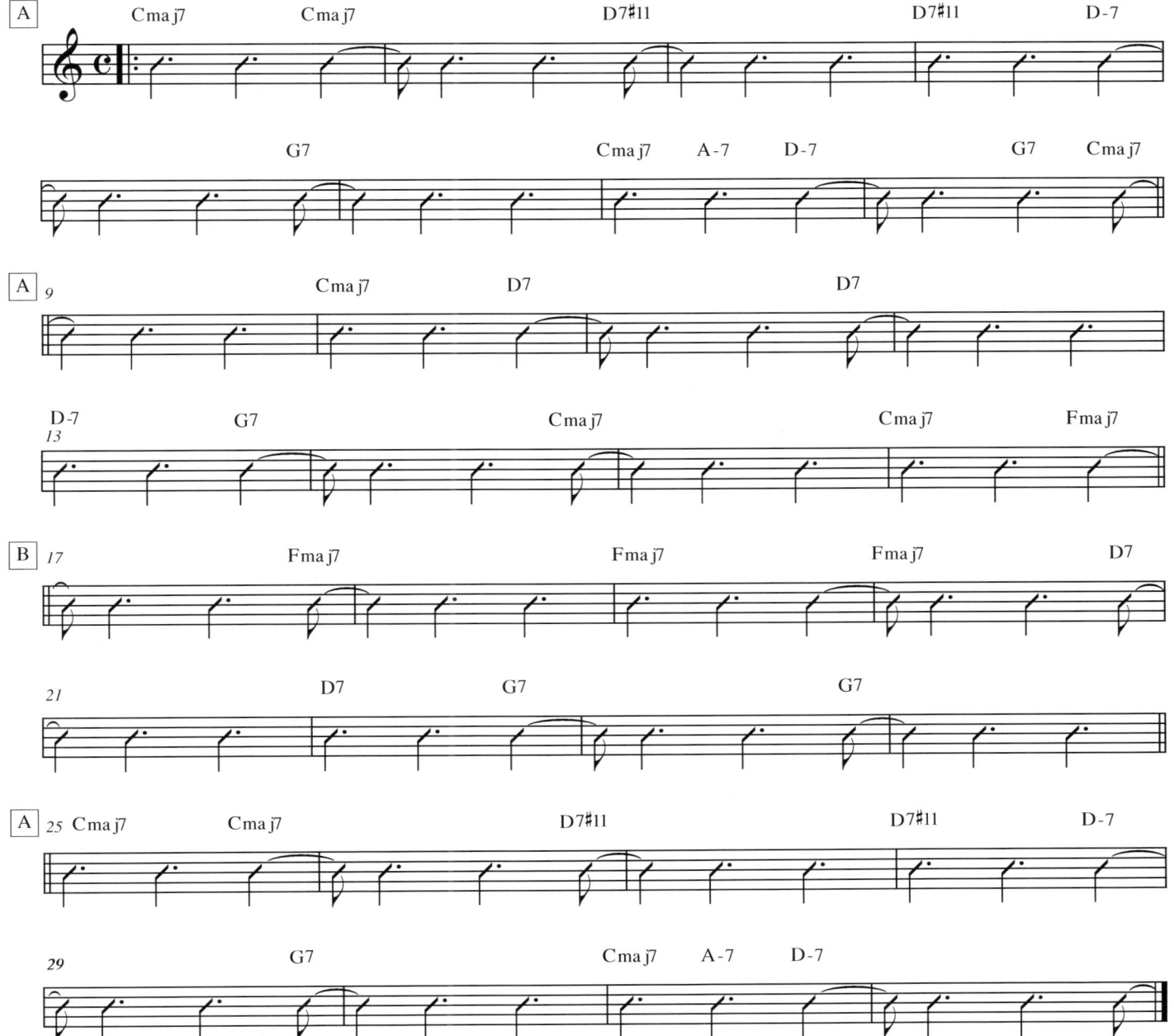

Here is a bass line for the same dotted quarter core rhythm.

Take the G Train

Chapter 34 from the section on quarter-note triplets. The **Core Rhythm** is a displaced quarter-note triplet in groupings of four and the form is a blues.

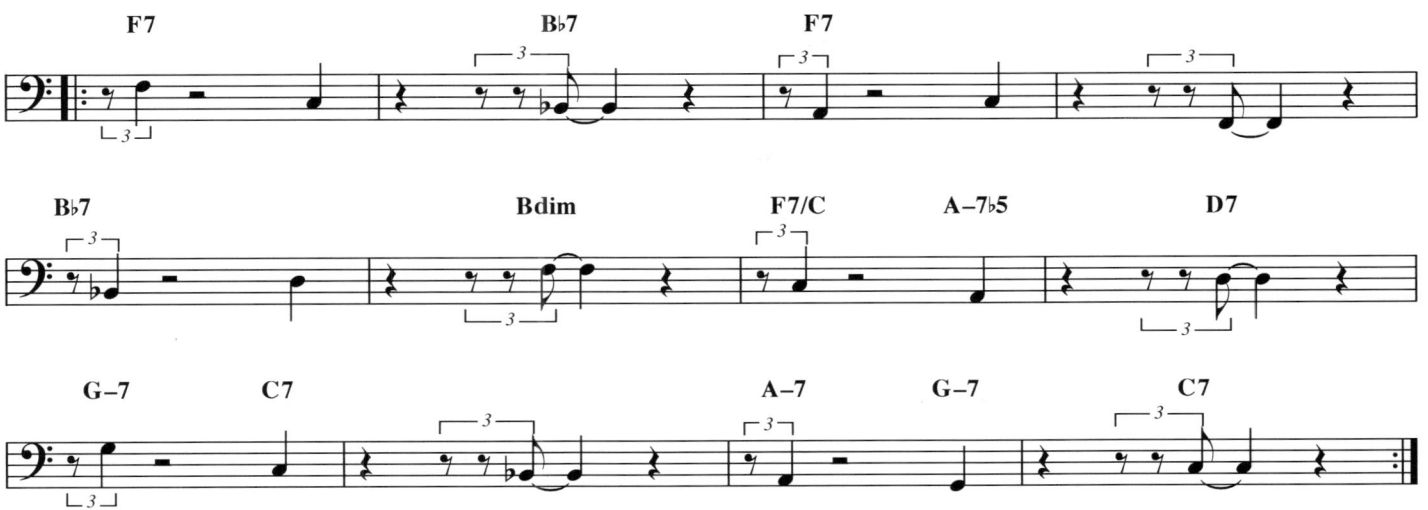

Below is the same example but with **Core Groove C**: Funk.

chord progressions

Blues in F

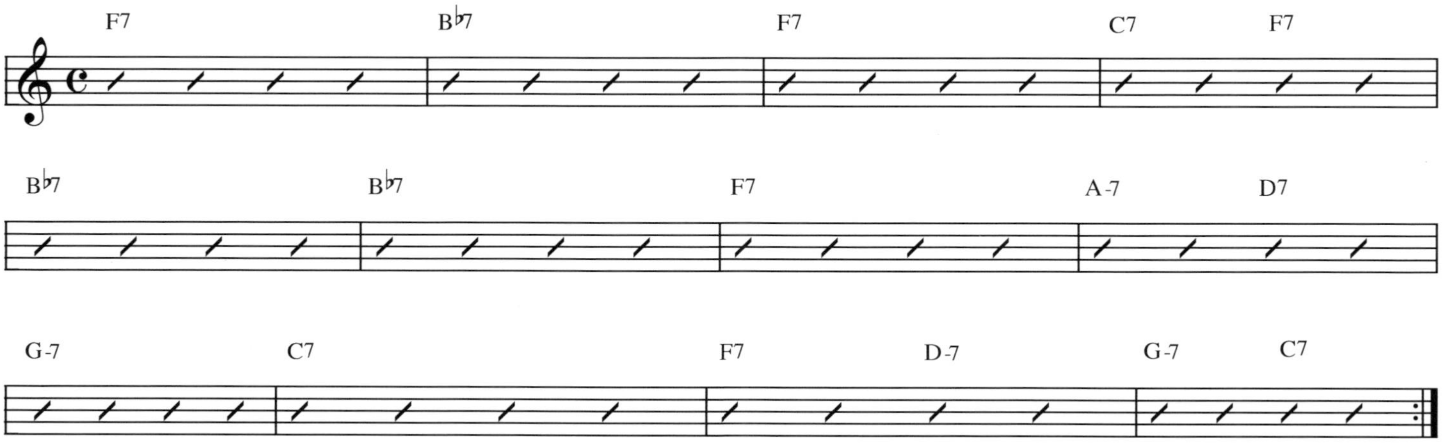

F7	B♭7	F7	C7 F7
B♭7	B♭7	F7	A-7 D7
G-7 C7	F7 D-7	G-7 C7

Pawprints

3/4

C-11	C-11	F-11	F-11
C-11	C-11	C-11	C7♭9
F-11	F-11	F-11	F-11
C-11	C-11	C-11	C-11
D-7♭5	D-7♭5	G7♭9	G7♭9
C-11	C-11	D-7♭5	G7♭9

Take the G Train

Rhythm Changes

suggested listening

Are you looking for musical examples of metric modulation?

Virtually every recording of the second great Miles Davis quintet between 1963 and 1968 contains examples of metric modulation. Here are just a few suggestions:

Miles Davis:	Miles Smiles
Miles Davis:	My Funny Valentine
Miles Davis:	Nefertiti
Miles Davis:	Four and More
Miles Davis:	The Sorcerer

Since then, metric modulation has become an integral part of the jazz vocabulary. You can find it on a majority of the recordings released since 1990. Here are some examples:

Wynton Marsalis:	Standard Time Vol. I
Wynton Marsalis:	Live at Blues Alley
Kenny Werner:	Form and Fantasy
Kenny Werner:	Peace
Kenny Werner:	Beat Degeneration
Ari Hoenig:	The Painter
Ari Hoenig:	Inversations
John O'Gallagher:	Axiom
Jochen Rueckert:	Introducing Jochen Rueckert
Ari Hoenig:	Bert's Playground

about the authors

Johannes Weidenmueller

Bassist Johannes Weidenmueller has been a member of Ray Barretto's New World Spirit, the Carl Allen–Vincent Herring quintet, the John Abercrombie quartet, the Joe Lovano trio and the Kenny Werner trio among others. Other associations include Benny Golson, James Moody, Gary Bartz, Clifford Jordan, Dewey Redman, Randy Brecker, Kenny Wheeler, Toots Thielemans, George Benson, Wynton Marsalis, Joshua Redman, Jonny Coles, Joe Chambers, Norah Jones, Madeleine Peyroux and many others. Johannes has appeared on over 60 recordings as a sideman. He has been on the faculty of the New School's jazz and contemporary music program in New York since 1997 where he teaches bass and ensemble. He is an in-demand clinician who gives lectures and workshops at universities and colleges around the world.

Ari Hoenig

Drummer Ari Hoenig was born in 1973 in Philadelphia, PA. He has worked extensively in bands led by Shirley Scott, Jean Michel Pilc, Kenny Werner, Chris Potter, Pat Martino, Joshua Redman, Wayne Krantz, Richard Bona, Mike Stern, Kurt Rosenwinkel, Bojan Z, Jazz Mandolin Project and James Hurt. Since 2002, Ari has been leading his own group in New York City where they play regularly at "Smalls" jazz club on Monday nights. Ari is a Dreyfus recording artist who has recorded five CD's and a live DVD as a leader. He is also on more than 80 recordings as a sideman. As an educator, Ari teaches privately in Brooklyn and also for the New School for Social Research in Manhattan. He gives clinics and lectures at music schools and universities worldwide and writes a regular educational column for *Modern Drummer* magazine.